225-YEAR-OLD KOIS!

By Joni Kelly

Gareth Stevens
PUBLISHING

Please visit our website, www.garethstevens.com. For a free color catalog of all our high-quality books, call toll free 1-800-542-2595 or fax 1-877-542-2596.

Cataloging-in-Publication Data

Names: Kelly, Joni.
Title: 225-year-old-kois! / Joni Kelly.
Description: New York : Gareth Stevens Publishing, 2019. | Series: World's longest-living animals | Includes index.
Identifiers: ISBN 9781538216941 (pbk.) | ISBN 9781538216934 (library bound) | ISBN 9781538216958 (6 pack)
Subjects: LCSH: Ornamental fishes–Juvenile literature. | Fishes–Juvenile literature.
Classification: LCC QL617.2 K45 2018 | DDC 597'.03–dc23

Published in 2019 by
Gareth Stevens Publishing
111 East 14th Street, Suite 349
New York, NY 10003

Designer: Andrea Davison-Bartolotta and Laura Bowen
Editor: Joan Stoaltman

Photo credits: Cover, p. 1 chuyuss/Shutterstock.com; pp. 2–24 (background) Dmitrieva Olga/Shutterstock.com; p. 5 Juriah Mosin/Shutterstock.com; p. 7 (top) Rostislav Stefanek/Shutterstock.com; p. 7 (bottom) Nuttapong Jeenpadipat/Shutterstock.com; p. 9 (fish) Khumthong/Shutterstock.com; p. 9 (background) scubaluna/Shutterstock.com; p. 11 Tom Black Dragon/Shutterstock.com; p. 13 Tamonwan_Newnew/Shutterstock.com; p. 15 Patrick Foto/Shutterstock.com; p.17 bluehand/Shutterstock.com; p. 19 GEORGES GOBET/AFP/Getty Images; p. 21 Sukpaiboonwat/Shutterstock.com.

Printed in the United States of America

CPSIA compliance information: Batch #CS18GS: For further information contact Gareth Stevens, New York, New York at 1-800-542-2595.

CONTENTS

Boldface words appear in the glossary.

Living Works of Art

If you've ever seen a koi (KOY) pond, you already know why these fish are called "living **jewels**" and "living works of art." The brightly colored kois—or *nishikigoi* (NEE-shee-kee-goy) in Japanese—are loved all over the world!

What Are Kois?

Kois are an **ornamental** fish farmers raise for people to keep! Kois' colors, **patterns**, size, and even shape come from hundreds—maybe even thousands—of years of **breeding**. Kois are a kind of carp. Carp have been in Japan for 5 million to 25 million years!

COMMON CARP

KOI

All kois have similar body and tail shapes. Because they're **cold-blooded**, they can live in warm or cool water. Kois can be 14 to 24 inches (36 to 61 cm) long. The largest koi ever, Big Girl, was 48 inches (122 cm) long and 90 pounds (41 kg)!

THE PARTS OF A KOI FISH

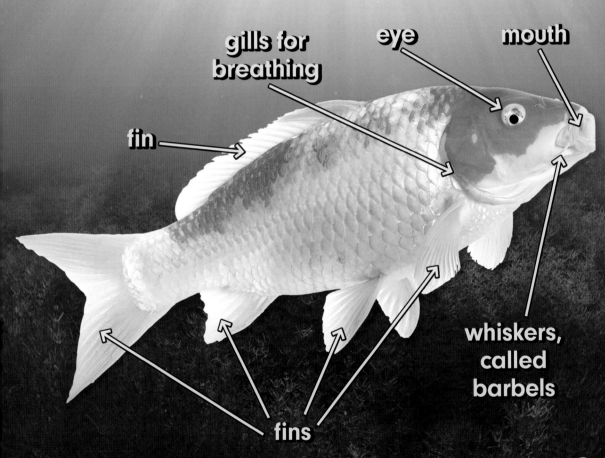

gills for breathing

eye

mouth

fin

whiskers, called barbels

fins

Bright colors on fish are easy for predators to see, but people love them! People especially love red, white, and yellow kois. There are 10 to 20 varieties, or groups, of kois, depending on whom you ask. Plus, there are over 200 names for different patterns and color mixes!

Hanako

The longest-living fish ever was likely a koi named Hanako. This bright red fish lived in a cold pond near a mountain in Japan for 226 years! Its age was figured out in 1966 using a **microscope** to study its **scales**.

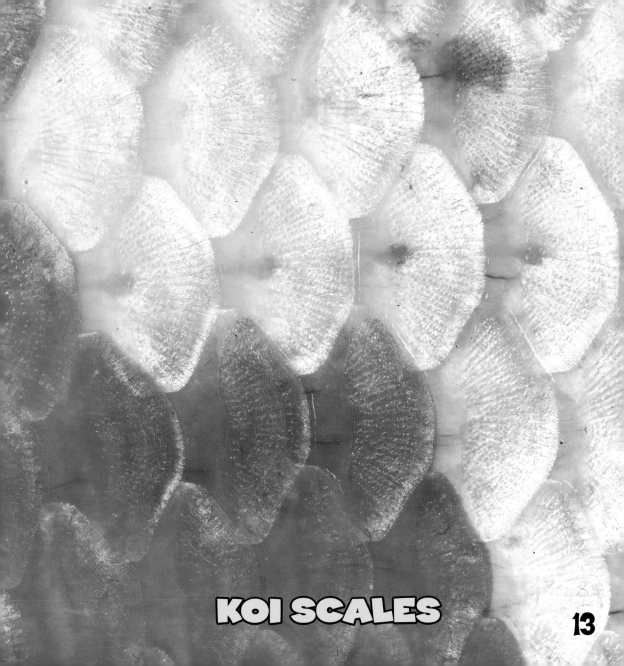

KOI SCALES

13

No one knows exactly how Hanako lived so long! The other kois in its pond all lived at least 139 years. Was it their cold pond? The clean mountain water? Or both? Special care from the family that owned them likely helped, too!

Koi Life

Kois don't usually live as long as Hanako. Many live to 50, though—which is still a long life for a fish! In the muddy ponds beneath mountains in Japan, they live around 70 years. Fish that live long are bred carefully to pass that **feature** on.

Japanese Kois Live Longer!

Kois raised in Japan live twice as long as everywhere else! Elsewhere, people make their kois grow quickly with food. Japanese kois rest in icy ponds every winter. This is called "wintering." Though they don't grow at all while wintering, this helps them live longer.

A Million-Dollar Fish?

A beautiful koi can be worth a lot of money. Big Girl cost about $40,000. A shiny, gold-colored koi once cost $2.2 million. The 2012 world **champion** koi cost more than $250,000. Well-bred kois are kept like famous paintings. Kois are truly living works of art!

GLOSSARY

breeding: the act of bringing together animals to produce babies that have certain features like color, pattern, or size

champion: someone who was judged to have won over others

cold-blooded: having a body that can be hot or cold based on where it is

feature: an interesting or important part, look, or way of being

jewel: something that is highly valued

microscope: a tool that makes a much larger view of very small objects so they can be seen clearly and studied

ornamental: used for its beauty

pattern: the way colors or shapes happen over and over again

scale: one of the many small, thin plates that cover the bodies of some animals

FOR MORE INFORMATION

BOOKS

Hamilton, S. L. *Fish*. Minneapolis, MN: ABDO Publishing Co., 2014.

Holmes, Keith, and Tony Pitham. *The World of Koi: Comprehensive Coverage, from Building a Koi Pond to Choosing Color Varieties*. Hauppage, NY: Barron's Educational Series, 2005.

WEBSITES

Japanese Koi
nationalzoo.si.edu/animals/japanese-koi
Check out the National Zoo's page about kois.

Koi Story
koistory.com/koi-fish-images/
Go here to see many beautiful pictures of kois.

Koi Variety Guide
blueridgekoi.com/koi-goldfish-resources/koi-variety-guide/
Read and see pictures of 24 different kinds of koi.

INDEX